LONELY LOVE

LONELY LOVE

LONELY LOVE

THE RIGHT OF NATASHA LAKSHMI TO BE IDENTIFIED AS THE AUTHOR OF THIS WORK HAS BEEN ASSERTED BY HER IN ACCORDANCE WITH THE COPYRIGHT, DESIGNS AND PATENTS ACT 1988.

ALL RIGHTS RESERVED. NO PART OF THIS PUBLICATION MAY BE REPRODUCED, STORED IN OR INTRODUCED INTO A RETRIEVAL SYSTEM, OR TRANSMITTED, IN ANY FORM, OR BY ANY MEANS (ELECTRONIC, MECHANICAL, PHOTOCOPYING, RECORDING OR OTHERWISE) WITHOUT THE PRIOR WRITTEN PERMISSION OF THE AUTHOR. ANY PERSON WHO DOES MAY UNAUTHORIZED ACT IN RELATION TO THIS PUBLICATION MAY BE LIABLE TO CRIMINAL PROSECUTION AND CIVIL CLAIMS FOR DAMAGES.

13 15 17 19 18 16 14 12

THIS BOOK IS SOLD SUBJECT TO THE CONDITION THAT IT SHALL NOT, BY WAY OF TRADE OR OTHERWISE, BE LENT, RE-SOLD, HIRED OUT, OR OTHERWISE CIRCULATED WITHOUT THE AUTHOR'S PRIOR CONSENT IN ANY FORM OF BINDING OR COVER OTHER THAN THAT IN WHICH IT IS PUBLISHED AND WITHOUT A SIMILAR CONDITION INCLUDING THIS CONDITION BEING IMPOSED ON THE SUBSEQUENT PURCHASER.

COPYRIGHT © NATASHA LASKHMI 2010

LONELY LOVE

NATASHA LAKSHMI

LONELY LOVE

FOR, ALL THE WOMEN IN THE WORLD WHO UNDERSTANDS AND KNOWS WHERE THIS STORY IS COMING FROM.

LONELY LOVE

CHAPTER 1
FUNKY FREE

PEOPLE ACROSS THE WORLD COME TO VISIT THE MOST FAMOUS CITY NEW YORK.
AN INDIAN GIRL NAMED SONYA WHO LIVES IN THE BUSY CITY WAS A FUN, HAPPY AND BEAUTIFUL WOMAN, BUT THERE WAS SOMETHING MISSING IN HER LIFE... LOVE.
IT WAS A MONDAY MORNING AND THE SUN WAS SHINING IN NEW YORK CITY, SONYA A BEAUTIFUL 27 YEAR OLD LIVES IN A 2-BEDROOM APARTMENT NEAR THE CITY, SHE WAS IN THE KITCHEN DRINKING HALF A CUP OF WARM COFFEE, SHE HAD BROWN EYES WITH SHOULDER LENGTH BLACK HAIR AND A SLIM BUILD, SHE WAS WEARING A RED V-NECK T-SHIRT WITH RED SHORTS WITH WHITE NIKE TRAINERS ON. SUDDENLY SHE SHOUTS IN THE KITCHEN "MUM"
SONYA'S MUM JENNY A MIDDLE-AGED WOMAN WITH LONG BLACK HAIR AND BROWN EYES AN AVERAGE BUILD, WEARING A WHITE V-NECK TOP WITH BLACK TROUSERS AND BLACK SHOES. SHE WAS IN SONYA'S BEDROOM TIDING UP THE MESSY BED AND FOLDING THE DUVET, SHE SUDDENLY STEPS ON A RED FANCY BRA AND SHE BENDS DOWN TO PICK IT UP WITH HER HANDS, WHEN SHE SEES SOMETHING FROM UNDER THE BED.
JENNY REACH HER HAND OUT FROM UNDER THE BED AND SHE GRABS A MAGAZINE OUT TO LOOK, IT WAS A GIRLS & GIRLS ISSUE AND SHE WAS HORRIFIED, SHE FREAKS OUT AND SHE SHOUTS IN THE ROOM "SONYA!"

THE NEXT THING SONYA AND JENNY WERE IN THE LOUNGE AND

Lonely Love

They both sat on the sofa next to each other.
Jenny wasn't happy with Sonya and she says to her "Why. Why be like this."
Sonya says to Jenny "I'm a lesbian."
Jenny looks at Sonya and she was shocked that her daughter fancied girls.
Jenny says to Sonya "You can't be one of those. How can you have children."
Sonya says "Mum please. Please relax."
Jenny says "Relax."
Jenny goes mad and she's infuriated and she says to Sonya "My daughter has told me that she is a lesbian and why should I relax."
Jenny gets up from the sofa and she picks up the cushion in front of her, she throws it at Sonya with frustration and she leaves the lounge.
Sonya says to Jenny "Mum where are you going?"
Jenny says "I'm going out."
Jenny walks up to the front door Sonya watches her across the room as her mother leaves the apartment.
Jenny wanted to get away from her daughter as it was causing her emotional stress to her; she walks in the street alone thinking long and hard about what she was going to do.
Sonya was in her apartment in the lounge standing near the window watching Jenny walking in the street upset; she wanted to go and stop her mother's sadness and to give her the warmth and love.

Later that afternoon Jenny was at the embankment and she was sat on the bench crying and whimpering and she says to herself "Why. Why me god."
Sonya was walking along the embankment and she sees her mother sat on the bench looking miserable; she walks up to

Lonely Love

HER LOOKING WORRIED AND CONCERN.
Sonya says to Jenny "Mum I've been looking for you."
Sonya sits next to Jenny and they both look at each other.
Jenny says to Sonya "Now I know why you came to help me organize family parties. So you can chat to the cute women."
Jenny cries and Sonya tries to calm her down and she puts her arm around to comfort her.
Sonya says to Jenny "I love you mum. I don't want to hurt you. I want you to be happy for me."
Jenny was shocked and she goes historical with her daughter's mad behaviour and she says "Happy! How can I be happy!"
Jenny quickly clams down and she has an idea for her daughter to be with a man and she says to Sonya "Can't you be with a man and then in the bedroom you can tell him to dress up as a woman."
Sonya freaks out listening to her mum's mad idea and she says to Jenny "Think about it. Decide if you want your daughter or not."
Sonya gets up from the bench and she walks away from her mother, leaving her to decide and think about weather they will keep there mother and daughter relationship.
Later that night Sonya was at her apartment in the lounge standing near the window, looking at her mobile in her hand and waiting for her mum's call and she was worried sick about her but she knew that she had to give Jenny time.
Suddenly Sonya hears the front door open and shut and Jenny walks into the lounge looking cool and calm about the situation.
Sonya looks at her mother waiting for an answer about there relationship.

Lonely Love

Jenny says to Sonya "I want my daughter."
Sonya gives a smile and she was so pleased that her mum approved with her sexuality, and she goes up to Jenny and they both give each other a hug.
Jenny looks at Sonya and she says to her "When can I see your girlfriend."
Sonya says to Jenny "I don't have one."
Jenny says "Your looking."
Sonya says "Yes."
Sonya turns her face away from Jenny and she says quietly "And having fun."
Jenny says "Come on. Let's have dinner."
Jenny walks to the kitchen and Sonya was glad to have her mum on her side.
Later that night Sonya was in her bedroom lying on the bed looking happy, she sits up and she turns around to take out a girls & girls magazine out from under the pillow to read.
Jenny was in her bedroom lying on the bed crying quietly, holding a photo of Sonya in her hand saying to herself "Why. Oh why be a lesbian."

As the night was passing by in New York City morning came, Sonya was in the lounge lying on the sofa watching the news channel, Jenny walks in and she goes up to the coffee table to pick up the remote control, she presses the red button to switch the T.V off.
Sonya says to Jenny "Mum I was watching that."
Sonya sits up from the sofa and Jenny looks at her and she says to her "I'm organizing a party for my friend. And I thought if you could come and help me."
Sonya says "Ok."
Sonya gets up from the sofa and Jenny says to her "And that doesn't mean you chase every woman there."

Lonely Love

Sonya says "Mum. I'm picky with women."
Jenny says "That's good. Come along."
Later that afternoon in Manhattan there was an Indian family party, Jenny was sorting out the decorations and Sonya was standing near the table, where the Indian food & soft drinks where laid, she was staring at a 26 year old woman with black eyes with black long hair slim build wearing a glamorous orange sari who was talking to two early 30-year-old men whom were smartly dressed.
Jenny sees Sonya's behaviour and she goes up to her and she says "Who are you looking at?"
Sonya looks at her mum and she says "I was.."
Jenny says "The woman you are looking at is married to one of them. Come and help me."
Jenny grabs Sonya's hand and she says to her "You can play later."

A few hours later the party had finished and the sun was going down in the busy city, Jenny and Sonya were both walking together in Wall Street, looking tired and exhausted after preparing the party all day.
Jenny says to Sonya "Did you find anyone you like?"
Sonya says "No. Some of them were married or engaged. They weren't lesbians."
Jenny says "You'll find someone. Even though I still haven't got over the fact you're a lesbian."
Sonya looks at her mum and she says to her "I thought you were ok about it."
Jenny says "I am. Let's just get home and relax."
Later that evening Jenny's elder brother Ravi a middle aged man with short black hair, clean shaven wearing a blue shirt and black trousers and black shoes, was round Sonya's apartment and he was in the lounge sat next to Jenny on the sofa.

Lonely Love

Ravi says to Jenny "Where's Sonya?"
Jenny says "She's gone out."
Ravi says "I know your upset that Sonya hasn't found a man."
Jenny comes out with Sonya's problems and she needed to talk to someone about it and she says to Ravi "My daughter has told me that she is a lesbian."
Ravi was shocked and he freaks out and he says "What! Girls of today they just want to be modern."
Jenny cries and she felt painfully self-conscious about, her daughter being a lesbian and she says to him "I love Sonya."
Ravi says "You know I'm here for you. You're my sister."
Jenny looks at Ravi and she says to him "Thank you. I need your support right now."
Ravi gives Jenny a hug to show his love and support and he wanted to help his sister.
Sonya was in the city and she was outside the coffee shop holding a plate of egg mayo sandwich in her hand, she goes to sit down at a small round table to eat her sandwich, a 18 stone white American 30 year old woman with brown eyes and short brown hair, wearing a black and white striped top with white trousers and white shoes was sat near her looking at her.
Sonya was about to eat her sandwich when she sees the big woman staring and smiling at her, she freaks out and she says quietly to herself "That's a one big mama."
Sonya gets up from her chair and she takes her sandwich of the plate and she walks off as quickly as possible.
Later that night Jenny was at the apartment wondering around the lounge waiting for her daughter to come home, she looks at the clock that was hanging on the wall and it was half past eleven.

Lonely Love

Jenny says "When is that girl coming home."
Jenny gives up waiting for Sonya and she was tired and she leaves the lounge, she goes to her bedroom to sleep.

It was 8 o'clock in the morning a 27-year-old woman with blue eyes, long blonde hair and a slim build, was wearing a black sexy underwear comes out of the kitchen holding half a glass, of cold orange juice that was from the fridge and she goes to Sonya's room.
Jenny comes out of her room wearing a baby blue salwar khamzee with sliver sandals and she goes in the kitchen and she shouts "SONYA!"
Jenny leaves the kitchen and she walks to Sonya's room and she knocks on the door and she says "Wake up."
Sonya was in her bedroom and she was wearing a black addias tracksuit, the woman was sat on the bed and she says "Who's that?"
Sonya was panicking and she says "It's my mum. You have to go."
The woman puts her jeans on and a red v-neck top on and she says to Sonya "Can I see you again?"
Sonya says "I'll phone you."
Sonya goes up to the door and she opens it, to see if her mum was wondering around, Jenny was in the kitchen washing the dishes and the woman walks out of the room and she goes to the front door.
Sonya follows and the woman gives, her a kiss on the cheek and she says "Bye."
The woman opens the front door and she walks out and Sonya shuts the door, Jenny hears her and she walks out of the kitchen and she says "Why are you standing at the front door?"
Sonya says "I was looking to see if we had any letters."
Sonya walks up to her mum looking guilty.

Lonely Love

Jenny says to Sonya "You came late last night."
Sonya says "I was with my friends."
Sonya keeps her cool and Jenny knew she was hanging out with a girl and she says "Did you bring someone home last night?"
Sonya was shocked and she looks away from her mum, it was like she wanted hide in a box, so no one could know her sexual feelings towards women.
Sonya says to Jenny "Why do you say that."
Jenny says "I heard a scream."
Sonya quickly thinks of an excuse to say.
Sonya says "I was scared."
Jenny says "Then you should have woken me up. If you were scared."
Sonya says "I'm hungry let's have breakfast."
Sonya walks to the kitchen ending her conversation with her mum about last night.
Later that afternoon in Manhattan one of the Indian neighbourhoods was having a garden party, Jenny was holding a plate full of mix Indian sweets, she places it on the table where the other few dishes were.
Sonya was walking around looking bored and tired, a few 6-year-old boys and girls were playing with two red balloons.
Jenny sees Sonya wondering around looking fed up, she gets annoyed with her daughter's laziness.
Jenny says "This girl will never find someone wondering around like that."
Suddenly Sonya sees her mum looking at her, she gives Jenny a wave to say that she was enjoying the party.
Later that night Jenny was at the apartment sat at the dinner table, she was on the pink Sony lap top looking for a lesbian woman on the net.
Jenny says to herself "If Sonya is not going to bother

finding a woman. Then I will."

Is Jenny making the right decision for finding a girl for Sonya?

CHAPTER 2
MIX MATCH

LA WHERE PEOPLE FROM ALL OVER THE WORLD, VISIT THE MAGNIFICENT CITY THAT HAS THE DREAM OF HOLLYWOOD. WHERE THEY HAVE THE BEST GAY NIGHTLIFE LOCATIONS TO GO AND TO DANCE IT UP, TO HAVE A DRINK AND GET SOME DELICIOUS FOOD AND MEET SEXY HOT PEOPLE.
SONYA WAS AT A BEACH PARTY AND SHE WAS WEARING A BLACK SEXY BIKINI TOP WITH SHORTS, SHE WAS CHATTING TO A 25 YEAR OLD WOMAN WITH BROWN EYES BLACK SHOULDER LENGTH HAIR, A SLIM BUILD WEARING A WHITE BIKINI TOP WITH WHITE SHORTS. SUDDENLY SONYA'S MOBILE WAS RINGING IN HER HAND AND SHE ANSWERS IT.
BACK IN NEW YORK JENNY WAS AT HOME AND SHE WAS STANDING NEAR THE DINNER TABLE, LOOKING AT THE SONY LAP TOP AND HOLDING THE MOBILE IN ONE HAND.
SONYA SAYS OVER THE PHONE "HELLO MUM."
JENNY SAYS "HELLO SONYA. WHAT ARE YOU UP TO?"
SONYA SAYS "I'M IN RESTAURANT WITH MY FRIENDS."
JENNY SAYS "OH YOUR IN A RESTAURANT WITH FRIENDS. SO HOW COME I CAN SEE YOU."
SUDDENLY SONYA WAS SHOCKED AND SHE QUICKLY LOOKS AROUND TO SEE WHERE HER MUM WAS, ALL SHE COULD SEE WAS MEN AND WOMEN DANCING TO RNB MUSIC.
SONYA SAYS "I DON'T BELIEVE THIS."
JENNY SAYS "YOUR AT A BEACH PARTY."
SONYA SAYS "HOW DO YOU KNOW."
JENNY GOES HISTORICAL OVER THE PHONE AND SHE SAYS TO SONYA "I'M WATCHING YOU ON THE LAP TOP. YOU FOOL. WHEN ARE YOU COMING HOME?"
SONYA SAYS "SOON."

Lonely Love

Jenny says "Soon means next week."
Jenny cries over the phone and she cuts the call off, Sonya looks at her mobile and she couldn't believe her mum's mad behaviour.

As the sun was going down in rocking LA, New York was missing out all the fun and a few days later, Sonya arrived home and she was at her apartment and she was outside, the terrace garden sat at the table next to Jenny and they were both looking at the Sony lap top, going throw a list of lesbian women on the net.
Sonya wasn't interested and she turns her nose, she says to Jenny "I don't like them."
Jenny says to Sonya "I thought you're a lesbian."
Sonya says "I am."
Jenny says "I've set you a date with a few of them. And this evening is your first date."
Sonya was stunned that her mother wanted to get involved in her love life.
Sonya says "What. Why mum."
Jenny says "You'll thank me later."
Jenny was happy that she could help her daughter find a woman, she gets up from chair looking pleased with herself and she walks inside. Sonya was sat there panicking and looking stress, about her date for this evening and she says to herself "What do I. I can't even run away."

Later that afternoon Sonya was in her bedroom and she was standing in front of the bed, looking at the black and red dress's, she was thinking of which one to wear.
Sonya says to herself "I will wear the black."
Jenny pops into Sonya's room looking cheerful and says to her daughter "Have you decided what to wear?"
Sonya says "Yes."

Lonely Love

Jenny says "Great."
Jenny goes up to Sonya and she gives her hug.
The next thing Sonya was wearing her black dress with black high heel shoes, she was looking sexy and she was at the restaurant called Water's Edge, she was with a 27-year-old Indian woman named Suzy, she had black eyes and black long hair a medium build, she was wearing a black skirt with a black shirt and she looked beautiful.
Suzy and Sonya were both sat at the table, waiting to order and they both look at each other.
Suzy says to Sonya "So you're a brain surgeon."
Sonya was shocked and she knew, who's funny idea this was and she says quietly in a huff "Mum."
Sonya looks at Suzy and she says "I don't work. I haven't worked for a year."
Suzy says to Sonya "But you said last night that you also worked part time in a school."
Sonya couldn't believe that her mum, lied about her and she gets annoyed and she says "I hate kids."
Suzy was shocked and she didn't like Sonya's attitude, she says to her "I should go. I need to pick up my son from my parents."
Suzy gets up from the chair and she leaves the restaurant looking hacked off and a 18-year-old male, with brown short hair and blue eyes, tall an average build was a waiter and he goes up to Sonya and he says to her "Are you ready to order."
Sonya looks at the waiter and she says to him "Yes."
The next thing Sonya was at the park and she walking alone, suddenly her mobile rings in her hand and she answers it.
Sonya says over the phone "Hello."
It was Jenny and she was at home and she says over the phone "Hi Sonya how did it go?"

Lonely Love

Sonya says "It was awful."
Jenny says "Don't worry you have number 2 this evening."
Sonya says "I have another date."
Jenny says "Bye."
Jenny hangs up and Sonya didn't look happy, having her mum choosing a woman for her.

Later that evening Sonya was at her apartment and she was still wearing her black dress, she was standing in the lounge with her mum.
Sonya was ready to go out and Jenny looks, at her and she gives a smile.
Jenny says to Sonya "You look beautiful. If only you see a man."
Sonya says "Mum I'm going."
Sonya leaves the lounge and Jenny watches her leave the apartment.
The next thing Sonya was at the embankment standing alone waiting for her date, she gives up after half an hour and then she walks off in the street to go home, as she was walking alone she felt sad and lonely, it was like her heart was empty and there was, no one to fill her life with love.
A few hours later Sonya arrived at her apartment and she sees her mum, in the lounge lying on the sofa waiting for her.
Sonya says "Mum."
Jenny says to Sonya "How did it go?"
Sonya says to Jenny "She didn't turn up. I can find someone you know."
Jenny says "I'll look again in the net."
Sonya says "No mum."
Jenny says "How about Suzy?"
Sonya says "That date was horrible. I'm going to bed.

Lonely Love

Goodnight."
Jenny says "Goodnight Sonya."
Sonya walks into her bedroom to get change and Jenny sits up from the sofa, thinking of how she could make her daughter happy and she takes a deep sigh.

The next morning the sun was shining bright in New York City, Jenny and Sonya were both standing in the kitchen eating egg and toast.
Jenny says to Sonya "Are you doing anything today?"
Sonya says "Why?"
Sonya is holding half a piece of toast in her hand and he looks at her mum, she is quick to know what her plan is.
Sonya says to Jenny "No way mum. I am not going on a date again."
Jenny says "I know you want to meet a woman of your choice. And I know she is out there waiting for you."
Sonya says "Mum that's deep."
Jenny looks at Sonya and she says to her "But I don't want you to make a mistake in your life."
Jenny gets a glass from the top cupboard, Sonya stood there thinking of what her mum had just said to her.
Sonya wanted to be with someone but it had, to be love and to bring her happiness in her life.

Will Sonya meet her dream woman?

Or will it be a man who will fill Sonya's heart with love?

LONELY LOVE

CHAPTER 3
FALLING IN LOVE

LOVE. FALLING IN LOVE IS EASY. TELLING SOMEONE THAT YOU LOVE HIM OR HER CAN BE HARD.
BECAUSE YOU DON'T KNOW HOW THEY WOULD FEEL ABOUT YOU.
AND YOU WOULDN'T WANT TO HURT OR UPSET THEM.

SO WHAT DO YOU DO?

HOLD ON TO YOUR FEELINGS?

OR JUST WALK AWAY WITH AN EMPTY HEART?

JENNY AND SONYA WERE IN MANHATTAN AND THEY WERE ROUND RAVI'S 3-BEDROOM SEMI DETACHED HOUSE, THEY WERE IN THE LOUNGE SAT AT THE DINNER TABLE.
RANI A MIDDLE AGED WOMAN WITH BLACK EYES AND BLACK HAIR TIED UP IN A BUN, WEARING A PINK SALWAR KHAMZEE SUIT WITH SLIVER SANDALS CAME OUT OF THE KITCHEN, HOLDING A TRAY OF TWO CUPS OF HOT TEA AND A SMALL ROUND PLATE, OF INDIAN MIX SWEETS AND SHE WALKS TO THE DINNER TABLE.
JENNY LOOKS AT RANI AND SHE SAYS TO HER "YOU SHOULDN'T HAVE MADE TEA."
RANI SAYS "DON'T BE SILLY. YOU DON'T OFTEN COME ROUND."
JENNY AND SONYA BOTH PICK UP A HOT CUP OF TEA FROM THE TRAY, RANI SITS ON THE CHAIR AND SHE LOOKS AT THEM AND SHE SAYS "MY NIECE IS GETTING MARRIED NEXT MONTH. AND I THOUGHT IF YOU WOULD LIKE TO ORGANIZE THE PARTY."
JENNY SAY "I WOULD LOVE TO."
RANI SAYS "SOON SONYA WILL BE WANTING TO GET MARRIED."
SONYA HAD A SUDDEN FEELING OF FEAR, IN HER AND SHE LOOKS

at her mum.
Jenny says to Rani "It's Sonya's choice."
Rani says "My nephew is single."
Sonya quickly interrupts and she looks at Rani and she says "No really aunty. I'm not ready."
Rani says "You only have to ask. And I will find you a man."
Jenny says "Don't worry Rani we will come to you if we need to find a man."
Sonya and Jenny both pick up their warm cup of tea to drink, they both keep quite about themselves as Rani, was sat there gossiping about other people's affair & problems.
The next thing Sonya and Jenny were both walking in Central park in the street, they were both looking stressed and worried after seeing Rani.
Jenny says to Sonya "At least we told Rani."
Sonya says "We could have told her the truth."
Jenny says "We can't tell her. She will freak out."
Sonya says "So."
Jenny says "Let's just wait for a little while. And then we can tell her."
Sonya says "Are you happy?"
Jenny says "What do you mean by happy?"
Sonya says "With me. That your daughter is a lesbian. Are you embarrassed of me."
Jenny holds Sonya's hand to show her that she cares and loves her daughter.
Jenny says "I'm not ashamed of you. I love you Sonya."
Sonya wanted to hear that her mum was on her side and she puts her arm around her, while they were both walking together in the street.
Jenny's feelings for her daughter were true love, she did accept Sonya's sexuality and there was happiness, in their

Lonely Love

RELATIONSHIP BUT IT WASN'T ENOUGH.

A MONTH LATER RANI'S NIECE HAD AN ENGAGEMENT PARTY AT A MANSION IN MANHATTAN; THERE WAS A GARDEN PARTY FOR THE SPECIAL OCCASION.
SONYA WAS LOOKING GLAMOROUS AND SHE WAS WEARING A BLACK SARI, JENNY WAS WEARING A BABY BLUE SARI, WEARING A FEW GOLD BANGLES IN HER RIGHT ARM, THEY WERE BOTH STANDING NEXT TO EACH OTHER.
RANI WAS WEARING AN ORANGE SARI AND SHE SEES JENNY AND SONYA STANDING, SHE GOES UP TO THEM TO ASK HOW THEY WERE.
RANI SAYS TO JENNY AND SONYA "HOW ARE YOU BOTH."
JENNY SAYS "WERE FINE."
RANI SAYS "THAT'S GOOD. MY SISTER WILL FIND A MAN FOR SONYA."
SONYA LOOKED SCARED AND SHE PANICS AND SHE DOESN'T KNOW WHAT TO SAY TO RANI.
RANI SAYS TO SONYA "DON'T WORRY. I FIND YOU A NICE GUY."
SONYA SAYS TO RANI "BUT I DON'T WANT TO GET MARRIED."
SONYA GETS ANGRY WITH RANI AND SHE WALKS OFF IN A MOOD.
JENNY LOOKS AT RANI AND SHE SMILES, TO SHOW THAT THEY HAD NO PROBLEMS AT HOME.
JENNY SAYS TO RANI "SONYA'S JUST UPSET OF BEING ON HER OWN."
RANI SAYS "DON'T WORRY JENNY ABOUT YOUR DAUGHTER. SHE WILL BE MARRIED IN NO TIME."
RANI WALKS OFF AND JENNY STOOD THEIR ALONE, LOOKING TROUBLED AND UNSETTLED AND SHE SAYS QUIETLY "YOU'LL BE SHOCKED WHEN YOU REALLY FIND OUT FROM SONYA."
A FEW MINUTES LATER RANI WAS HOLDING A GLASS OF COKE IN HER HAND, SHE GOES UP TO JENNY TO GIVE TO HER.
RANI SAYS TO JENNY "ARE YOU ALRIGHT."
JENNY SAY "YES."

Lonely Love

Rani says "I'll show you a few men for you to choose for Sonya."

The next thing Sonya was walking around the garden, looking fed up and she had her head held down, it was weighing her down mentally and physically, with her relatives telling her to find a man and get married. Jenny was sat at the table with a few, other elderly men and women relatives, eating mix flavours of crisp's and drinking cups of fizzy drinks, she sees Sonya talking to Rani.
Jenny says quietly to herself "Here we go. Why is Rani harassing Sonya."
Rani says to Sonya "Why haven't you got a boyfriend?"
Sonya looks away from Rani and she ignores what she was saying to her.
Rani says to Sonya "You can tell me."
Sonya was getting irritated by, Rani's questions and any minute she was going to scream.
Rani says to Sonya "So tell me what kind of a man suits you. I know well educated and handsome men."
Suddenly Sonya was feeling extremely annoyed and angry looking like a devil.
Sonya shouts at Rani "I'M A LESBIAN!
Suddenly friends and relatives stop and stare at Sonya in shock, Jenny was sat at the table and she hides her face with her hand, she wanted to sink into her chair and disappear.
It made Rani feel horror and disgust and she says to Sonya "What!"
Sonya pretends to act normal like nothing hasn't happen and she walks off, Rani sees Jenny sat at the table looking anxious to know what has happened.
Rani goes up to Jenny to find out what is going on with

Lonely Love

Sonya's life.
Rani says to Jenny "Why didn't you tell me?"
Jenny was sat in her chair and she looks away from Rani, as she knew that know one, would not agree with homosexuality.
As Sonya was walking in a hurry as, family and friends were staring at her and talking about her sexuality, she ignores them and she carries on walking, when suddenly 25 year old woman named Pooja, had brown eyes and long black hair, a slim build wearing a pink glamorous sari with shinny sliver bangles in her arms.

Could this be the woman Sonya has been waiting for?

Sonya sees Pooja walking up to her, she could not believe her eyes she was beautiful.
Pooja looks at Sonya and they both smile, at each other and they both walk up to each other.
Sonya says "Hi I'm Sonya."
Pooja says "I'm Pooja."
Sonya and Pooja both shake each other's hand; this was a new beginning of friendship for the two of them.
Later that evening Sonya was at her apartment, she was in the lounge wearing her black nightclothes, she was sat on the sofa looking happy and cheerful, Jenny walks in and says to her "Who was that girl you were talking to this evening?"
Sonya says to Jenny "Her name is Pooja."
Jenny says "Pooja. She seems like a nice girl."
Sonya says "She is."
Jenny says "Rani was upset for me. But I ignored it. So when are you going to see Pooja."
Sonya says "Tomorrow."
Sonya looks at her mum standing in front of her, she

Lonely Love

gives her a smile to show that she is happy again, she gets up from the sofa and she leaves the lounge and she goes to her room.
Jenny was pleased to see her daughter's happiness and she sits on the sofa to watch T.V.

The next day it was an afternoon Sonya and Pooja were, both in the city walking in the park together.
Pooja says to Sonya "So you live with your mum. Does she know that you're a lesbian."
Sonya says "Yes she knows and she is happy for me."
Pooja was surprised that Sonya's mum was open minded about her sexuality.
Pooja says to Sonya "I wish my parents were like that."
Sonya giggles and Pooja links her arm with hers, they both carry on walking and there had a liking to each other.

As the days were going by Sonya and Pooja would often see each other, they would go out in the city, to have lunch and dinner to talk about there everyday life.
One afternoon Sonya was round Pooja's one bedroom apartment in the city.
Sonya and Pooja were both sat on the sofa, they both gaze into each other's eyes, there hearts were beating for one another, they go closer to each other and they have a passionate kiss.
The next thing Sonya and Pooja were both walking together at the embankment.
Sonya wanted to tell Pooja something and she had feelings for her.
Sonya says to Pooja "I love you."
Pooja turns to look at Sonya and she says to her "I love you too."

Lonely Love

Pooja and Sonya's love had just begun for one another, they were both happy together.
Later that evening Sonya was at her apartment, she was sat at the dinner table with her mum.
Jenny says to Sonya "Are you going to see Pooja this evening?"
Sonya gets the thrills hearing someone say Pooja's name, it would make her heart beat faster and she says to Jenny "Yes I am in love."
Sonya smiles and Jenny could see that her daughter was in love; suddenly they hear the doorbell ring.
Jenny gets up from the chair and she leaves, the lounge to answer the front door and it was Pooja.
Pooja says "Hello auntie."
Jenny says "Hello. You must be Pooja."
Pooja says "Yes."
Jenny gives Pooja a hug and welcomes her inside and Sonya sees them, she gets up from the chair and she quickly goes up to them.
Sonya says to Pooja "Shall we go out."
Pooja says "Ok."
Jenny says to Sonya "But the girl had just come in."
Sonya takes Pooja's hand and they both walked out, they shut the front door.
Jenny stood there inside with her hands on her hips and she says "That girl can be a hand full at times."
The next thing Sonya and Pooja were both walking together in South Street holding hands looking happy.
Pooja says to Sonya "I like your mum. She's nice. Sometimes I wish my mum could understand how I feel."
Sonya turns to look at Pooja, she felt sorry for her that she had no support from her family.
Sonya says to Pooja "Why don't you tell your mum."
Pooja says "I can't."

Lonely Love

Sonya says "Your scared."
Pooja was worried about how her parents finding out that she is a lesbian; it would constantly be on her mind.

Is someone going to be left with an empty heart?

Lonely Love

CHAPTER 4
DON'T GO

It's the middle of July and everyone in New York, was loving the hot summer but not for some.
Sonya was at her apartment and she was wearing her black nightclothes, she was in her bedroom sat on the bed thinking about Pooja's problems and worrying, about her parents finding out that, she is a lesbian and she takes a deep sigh.
Jenny was in the lounge and she was standing near the dinner table, holding a small bowl of corn flakes in her hand, she shouts across the room so Sonya could hear her.
Jenny shouts "Sonya aren't you coming to have breakfast?"
Sonya gets up from the bed and she leaves her room and walks in the lounge, Jenny was sat at the dinner table and she could see, her daughter looking stressed and worried about something.
Jenny says to Sonya "Are you alright?"
Sonya says "I'm fine."
Sonya goes to sit opposite Jenny and she picks up a piece of toast from the plate near her, she eats it slowly as she was sat there she felt like her heart, was soon going to be empty and was soon, to stop beating for the one she loved.

Pooja was at her apartment she was in the kitchen holding in her hand a written letter, from her parents saying to come home and her mobile rings on the table near her, she looks to see who's calling, it was Sonya and she didn't know what to do.

Lonely Love

Sonya was at her apartment and she was, standing outside the terrace looking at her mobile and she says "Why isn't Pooja answering?"

Sonya was looking worried and concern and she takes a deep sigh, she was confused and she couldn't understand why Pooja wasn't talking to her.

Pooja was at her apartment and she was taking her lightweight medium red suitcase to the front door, she gets her mobile out from her jeans pocket, she calls Sonya but there was no answer.

Sonya was at her apartment and she comes out of the bathroom and she walks to her room, she picks her mobile up from the bed to see if Pooja had phoned, she had a missed call from her.

Sonya says "Pooja."

Sonya quickly calls Pooja hoping that she would have a chance to talk to her girlfriend and ask her, what the problem was but there was no answer.

Jenny was holding a red washed v-neck t-shirt and she walks into Sonya's room.

Jenny says to Sonya "Here's your t-shirt."

Jenny looks at Sonya and she could see in her daughter's face what has happened.

Jenny says "Why don't you go and see Pooja. And sort things out with her."

Jenny goes up to Sonya and she gives her a hug to let her daughter know, the love and warmth and to tell her to hold on to the relationship with Pooja.

The next thing Sonya arrived at Pooja's apartment, she knocks on the front door to see if she is in.

Sonya says "Pooja. It's me Sonya."

Sonya stands there waiting for about 5 minutes and then she takes her mobile out, of her jeans pocket to call Pooja but it went onto answer message. She gives up and

Lonely Love

She walks off looking angry and upset.

Later that night Sonya was at her apartment and she was outside, the terrace taking some fresh air and she had her arms crossed, looking extremely annoyed that Pooja had broken her heart into small pieces, Jenny goes outside to see her.
Jenny says to Sonya "Talk to me. Tell me what's wrong?"
Sonya says "She left me. And she doesn't love me. She's hurt me."
Sonya had tears in her eyes and it had caused her a lot of pain, Jenny looks at her and they both hold on to each other.
Jenny couldn't bear seeing her daughter crying or being hurt and upset.
Jenny takes Sonya inside to calm down, as for them being outside having the stars shining up at the night sky, wasn't bringing them hope it made them more upsetting.

As the hours go pass in the night, the sun rises up to shine onto city of gloomy New York.
Sonya was at her apartment and she was in kitchen with her mum, they are both holding a cup of warm coffee.
Suddenly Sonya's mobile rings on the, dinner table and she quickly leaves the kitchen, holding on to her cup of coffee in her hand and she goes, to the dinner table to see her phone and it was Pooja.
Jenny walks out of the kitchen listening to her daughter's conversation, she was feeling anxious and concern and Sonya looks at her mum.
Sonya says over the phone "I have to go bye."
Sonya puts her mobile on the dinner table and she looks sad, as she takes a deep sigh of sorrow, as if her heart

Lonely Love

was been ripped into half, she felt an emotional strain in her life.

Jenny says to Sonya "Who was it?"

Sonya says "It was Pooja. She's in India and her parents have found her a man to get married to."

Sonya couldn't control her sadness and she cries, she had tears flowing down from her face she sits on the floor, it was like her love had been, torn apart and Jenny was watching her daughter suffering in pain.

While Jenny stood there in the lounge, she had never seen her daughter so upset and unhappy, only when her father passed away 11 years ago.

Jenny gave her daughter a lot of love and happiness, but even that is not enough for a child's heart.

Will Jenny and Sonya say goodbye to each other?

LONELY LOVE

CHAPTER 5
BRINGING YOU BACK

As the summer was coming to an end in New York City, autumn was soon to arrive, it wasn't going to bring happiness for one woman.
Sonya was at her apartment in the lounge lying, on the sofa holding a red cushion close to her chest, she was feeling low and depressed as she takes a deep sigh of loneliness, Jenny walks in holding a hot cup of coffee and she puts it on the table.
Jenny says to Sonya "I've made you a cup of coffee."
Sonya says "Thanks mum."
Jenny looks at Sonya's sad face and she says to her "I don't like to see you in pain and sorrow. You need to go and get Pooja before it's too late."
Sonya gets upset after listening to her mother's words, she was right what Jenny had said to her.

Sonya had to go and get her love.

But is she doing the right thing?

The next thing Jenny was in Sonya's room packing her daughter's clothes, into a small black suitcase that was on the bed.
Sonya walks into her room holding a small red bag, which had her toothbrush and toothpaste in, she puts it in the suitcase.
Sonya says to Jenny "Mum I was thinking that you should come with me."
Jenny says to Sonya "Are you sure you want me to come

with you."

Sonya says "I need your support. Please say yes."

Jenny says "Yes I will go with you. I will help you get Pooja."

Sonya was pleased that her mum was by her side and they give each other a hug to show their love.

As they leave dull New York City Sonya and Jenny were both going to India, where the sun was shining and people showing the colours of happiness there. But could it bring love and happiness to Sonya and Pooja?

New Delhi is the capital of India. You can buy silk products, precious stones, leather and woodworks there but the most important thing about Delhi, is that you can find almost anything from anywhere in the world.

Pooja was at her 5-bedroom house, which had a big front and back garden, that had a few benches to sit and relax.

Pooja was upstairs in her bedroom she was standing, near the open window looking up at the night sky, all she could think about was Sonya and how she wanted, to be with her and to tell her that she loved her very much.

Pooja was upset as her heart was yearning for something that she couldn't have, her father Dev a middle aged man with black eyes and black short hair, an average build wearing a blue shirt with brown trousers, with black shoes on walks into her room.

Dev says "Pooja."

Pooja turns around and she quickly hides her sadness away from her father, Dev goes up to her wanting to know why his daughter was upset.

Dev says to Pooja "Are you alright?"

Pooja says to Dev "I'm fine. Tell mum I'm coming down to look at the bridle clothes."

Dev says "You know you can talk to me."

Lonely Love

Pooja says "There's no problem dad."
Dev smiles at Pooja and he turns around and he leaves the room, Pooja stands there knowing that there was a problem, but for how long could she keep her secret for?

Sonya and Jenny were half an hour away from Pooja's house.
Jenny's younger sister Sangeeta lived in a 3-bedroom house that had a small front and back garden, she was divorced and she had a 22-year-old son, who was in the army fighting in Afghanistan.
Sangeeta had long black hair and black eyes a slim build wearing a dark blue salwar khamzee with blue sandals; she was in the lounge with her sister and niece.
Sangeeta says to them "I'm so happy that you've come to stay."
Sonya was feeling drowsy and she wanted to go to sleep, she was tired from the 8-½ hour flight and she says to Jenny "Mum I'm going upstairs to sleep."
Jenny says "Ok."
Sonya leaves the lounge and she walks up the stairs to her room where her small suitcase, was on the floor near the single bed.
Jenny and Sangeeta were standing near the sofa and they both look at each other.
Sangeeta wanted to know why her sister had really come to visit her.
Sangeeta says to Jenny "So why are you really here?"
Jenny says to Sangeeta "Sonya wanted to see someone."
Sangeeta says "Who? Has she come here to get married."
Jenny had no choice but to tell her sister the truth about Sonya.
Jenny says "My daughter is in love with a woman."
Sangeeta stood there in shock and she freaks out like it

Lonely Love

was disease, she sits on the sofa to calm down. Sangeeta says to Jenny "Your daughter is a lesbian." Jenny says "Yes and I don't want you to say anything to Sonya. She's already upset that Pooja is getting married."

Sangeeta kept quite and she didn't know what to say to her sister, weather Jenny was doing the right thing for Sonya.

One of the reasons is that those in the Asian community attracted, to the same sex cannot be open about it to their families due to the stigma attached in the, culture of being gay or lesbian it's a non-acceptance.

Being homosexual in the Desi culture, is a major struggle between family and child.

Many parents turn a blind eye and are convinced, that their son or daughter will grow out of it.

Many families disown many women, who have come out, because it is seen as bringing disrespect and shame on the family.

And some parents get them married to the opposite sex, hoping that they will become 'straight' once they are married.

But for Pooja she knew who she was and she wanted to come out of her shell, but people around her were stopping her of being who she was.

Will Pooja have the courage to see Sonya again?

As another day passes by in New Dehli Sonya was day dreaming she was ready to take Pooja, in her arms but it wasn't going to be easy.

The next morning Pooja and Sonya were both in Lodi garden

Lonely Love

It's a popular place for morning/evening walk or a jog, they were both walking together in the garden looking sad and distressed.
Pooja says to Sonya "Why did you come?"
Sonya says "Because I love you."
Pooja felt heart broken hearing that Sonya still wanted to be wit her.
Pooja says to Sonya "My parents have found a man for me. And tomorrow night is my engagement party."
Sonya wasn't happy that Pooja was going to be taken away from her.
Sonya says "Are you happy?"
Pooja gives attitude to Sonya and she gives her the cold shoulder.
Pooja says "Why does that matter."
Sonya expresses her extreme annoyance at Pooja and she says to her "It matters to me."
Pooja says "I have to go. Come tomorrow evening."
Pooja doesn't look at Sonya and she walks out of the Lodi garden, to get away from the mess she has in her life.
Suddenly Pooja's mother Asha a middle aged woman with black eyes and black hair, which was tied up in a bun and a curvy build was wearing, a plain pink sari with sliver sandals was, standing outside the shop looking at the different colours of fabric.
Pooja sees her mum and she quickly walks off, to a coffee shop so Asha could not see her.
Sonya walks out of Lodi garden alone full of sadness; she has her head held down and tears, in her eyes rolling down her cheeks. It was like there was no one was, on her side to help her get her love.
It was a busy day for Pooja's parents as, they both were organizing the party at their house, having a few people

cooking the food for tomorrow evening. Everything was all set but, Pooja was pretending to show her parents that she was happy.

As the sun was going down in New Dehli Sonya was at Sangeeta's house, she was in the kitchen with her mum both looking emotionally distressed.

Jenny says to Sonya "Don't get upset. Everything will be fine."

Sonya says "I don't know if it will be ok mum."

Jenny looks at Sonya and she touches her face and she says "It will trust me."

Jenny gives Sonya a hug to comfort her and to take her sadness away from her life.

Pooja was at home and she was in her room lying on the bed, thinking about how her life was going to be sad without Sonya, she had tears flowing down from her face but, she could not hide away her love for a woman.

As the night was passing by it soon came morning Jenny, Sonya and Sangeeta were at home, they were sat at the dinner table eating beans on toast.

Sonya wasn't eating her beans on toast she was sat there thinking, about Pooja and what she had said to her yesterday. It was like there relationship was coming to an end.

Pooja was at home and she was in the lounge lying on the sofa, thinking about how Sonya was ready to take her to New York, she takes a deep sigh of sorrow and she didn't want the day to end, because of her engagement party in the evening.

As the hours were going by Sonya and Pooja were both waiting to meet each other in the evening.

It was evening and Pooja's friends and relatives were round to celebrate the special occasion.

Lonely Love

Pooja was wearing a red glamorous sari with two gold bangles on each of her arms, a gold necklace and a sliver ring on her finger, she was standing next to her man a 28 year old, with black eyes and black short hair a slim athletic build, wearing a white shirt and black trousers with black shoes.

Pooja stood there with her man looking, to see when Sonya was coming to rescue her.

Sonya was at home and she was upstairs in her room, looking at her white glamorous sari that was on the bed, Jenny walks in and she sees her daughter is not ready to go to the party.

Jenny says to Sonya "Are you going to get ready?"

Sonya says "I'm not going."

Jenny says "Why?"

Sonya gets upset and she puts her hands, on her hips and says she's had enough of fighting for the one she loves.

Jenny goes up to Sonya and she puts her arm around her and she says "Go and see Pooja."

Sonya says to Jenny "Will you come with me."

Jenny says "If that's what you want."

Sonya looks at her mum and she holds her to say thank you.

The next thing Sonya and Jenny both arrived at Pooja's house, they see relatives having a good time and some of them were talking to Pooja.

Sonya was looking worried and scared; Jenny was walking with her to show her support for her daughter.

Jenny says to Sonya "You can do this."

Pooja, Dev and Asha walk up to Sonya and Jenny, as they were both new to the family.

Pooja says to Sonya "Hi."

Sonya says "Hi Pooja."

Pooja says to Jenny "Hello auntie."

Jenny says "Hello Pooja."
Pooja looks at her parents and she says to them "This is Sonya she is from New York. She's a good friend of mine."
Dev says to Sonya and Jenny "Hello."
Asha says to Sonya and Jenny "Hello"
Dev says to Sonya and Jenny "You both have to stay with us."
Sonya, Jenny and Pooja were shocked and it wasn't going to plan.
Jenny says to Dev "We can't."
Asha says to Jenny "What do you mean you can't. Come tomorrow with your things and you can both stay here till the wedding."
Dev says to Jenny and Sonya "You have to stay. You can't say no."
Pooja looks at her parents and she isn't happy and she says to them "Do you think it's a good idea."
Dev says to Pooja "Don't be silly. Sonya is your friend."
Pooja and Sonya both look at each other and it was like there love, for each other was soon going to come out for everyone, to know like a bomb waiting to explode.
The next morning Jenny was at Sangeeta's house and she was in the lounge, with her sister and there were two small black suitcases near, the front door waiting to go to Pooja's house.
Sangeeta says to Jenny "Where's Sonya?"
Jenny says "She's upstairs."
Sangeeta was being arrogant and she was not having it with Sonya's sexuality, she gives Jenny attitude and she says to her "I hope you know what you were doing to your daughter."
Jenny ignores Sangeeta's opinion and she says "I love my

Lonely Love

daughter. And if she wants to be with a woman she can."
Sangeeta says "It's not right."
Jenny says "For you it isn't. I'm glad that me and my daughter are not staying here with you."
Suddenly Sonya was standing at the top of the stairs listening to Jenny and Sangeeta's conversation, she covers her mouth with her hand and she cries quietly, so they could not hear her pain and sorrow.

Will the truth come out?

Will Sonya get her love before it's taken away from her?

Lonely Love

CHAPTER 6
ONE GIRL

New Dehli was celebrating a new beginning for Pooja, leaving New York alone with sadness and grief for Sonya. Sonya and Jenny were both at Pooja's house in the lounge; they were both standing next to their suitcases. Pooja walks down the stairs and she goes, into the lounge to see Sonya and Jenny.
Pooja says to them "Auntie. Sonya. Let me show you the room."
Pooja leaves the lounge and she goes upstairs, Jenny and Sonya both take their lightweight, small suitcases upstairs to the room.
Pooja was in the room with Jenny and Sonya and she says to them "If you need anything. Don't be scared to ask."
Jenny looks at Pooja and she says to her "You've already done enough for us. You don't need to worry about us."
Dev shouts from downstairs "POOJA."
Pooja says to Jenny "I should go downstairs. See you later."
Pooja and Sonya both didn't look at each other, as they were both scared of their feelings for one another.
Pooja leaves the room and she goes downstairs to find out what her dad wanted, Sonya looks around at the bedroom and she goes to sit on the double bed and she says to Jenny "What do I do?"
Jenny looks at Sonya and she says "Talk to her."
Sonya was fed up with Pooja's lack of enthusiasm and she takes a deep sigh.

The next thing Pooja was outside the terrace garden

Lonely Love

Holding a glass of water, in her hand for her grandfather a 70-year-old man named Yash, was sat on the chair and he had white short hair and black eyes, a slim build wearing grey trousers and a white shirt.
Pooja gives the glass of water to Yash, he takes it from her and he says "Thank you dear. I heard your friend has come to stay with us."
Pooja says "Yes."
Yash says "What's her name?"
Pooja says "Sonya."
Yash says "It's nice of you to invite Sonya to your wedding."
Pooja smiles at her grandfather and on the other hand she was thinking, of what was going to happen to her life in the next few days.
The next thing Pooja and Sonya were downstairs in the kitchen and they were both looked stressed.
Pooja says to Sonya "I still don't understand why you have come."
Sonya says "Like I said. I want you. I am in love with you."
Pooja was tired of listening to Sonya's feelings for her, it was like she wanted to run away from her sexuality.
Pooja says to Sonya "I don't believe this."
Sonya says "Your not getting married Pooja."
Pooja says "I have no choice."
Sonya was disappointed with Pooja and she couldn't understand why she wouldn't run away with her, she walks out of the kitchen in a bad mood.
Pooja says "Sonya."
Pooja was in the kitchen and she thought Sonya was being childish, about their situation and she wasn't being reasonable.

Lonely Love

Later that night Sonya was upstairs in the room with her mum and they were both sat on the bed, thinking about their next plan to save Pooja from the evil people around her.
Jenny says to Sonya "So when are you and Pooja running away?"
Sonya says "Pooja is not ready to go with me. I can't kidnap her."
Jenny says "She's scared."
Sonya says "I'm not."
Jenny says "Your not the one that's getting married."
Sonya looks at her mum wanting to know the right way for her plan.
Sonya says to Jenny "What do we do?"
Jenny says "I guess you will have to wait."
Sonya couldn't wait for Pooja to be with her, she was in two minds about saying goodbye to her.
The next thing Pooja was in her bedroom lying on the bed awake, Sonya opens the door and she walks in and she shuts the door.
Pooja sits up from the bed and she looks at Sonya.
Pooja says to Sonya "If you have come to take me away. You can forget it."
Sonya goes up to Pooja and she says "I know your scared."
Pooja says "I'm not scared."
Sonya says "You're a chicken."
Pooja says "I'm not a chicken. Can you go I want to sleep."
Sonya gives Pooja a kiss on the cheek and she says "Goodnight chicken."
Pooja says "Sonya!"
Pooja gets a pillow from behind her and she hits Sonya in the stomach, they were giggling and messing about and they

go closer to each other, as they both look into each other's eyes they have a passionate kiss. They could not keep their love away, from each other even though there relationship was at its last breath.

The next day Sonya and Yash were both outside in the garden and they were both sat on the bench, they were chatting to each other.

Yash says to Sonya "Do you have a boyfriend?"

Sonya says "No."

Yash says "Are you going to have an arrange marriage?"

Sonya says "Never."

Sonya couldn't keep her secret away from Yash and so she tells him.

Yash says "It's Pooja's wedding tomorrow. Are you excited?"

Sonya says "No."

Yash says "Why?"

Sonya says "Because I love her."

Yash sits there in shock and he freaks out and he gets up from the bench, he walks inside saying nothing to Sonya and she sits there outside, knowing that there's going to be trouble for her and Pooja the war begins.

Yash was in the lounge and he sees Pooja sat on the sofa watching, the music channel on T.V and he goes up to her and she looks at him.

Yash says to Pooja "We need to talk."

Pooja could see that her grandfather didn't look happy, he leaves the lounge and he goes upstairs to his room.

Pooja gets up from the sofa leaving the T.V on and she leaves the lounge, she goes upstairs to her grandfather's room where he was sat on the bed looking very stressed.

Pooja couldn't work out what was wrong with her grandfather, she then thought it might be the wedding and her saying goodbye to her family.

Lonely Love

Yash gets up from the bed and he walks around the room trying to find out if Sonya is telling the truth, Pooja walks in the room looking worried and anxious.
Yash looks at Pooja and he says to her "Do you love Sonya?"
Pooja is horrified and she stands still like a block of ice slowly to melt.
Yash says to Pooja "Don't be with a woman. It's wrong."
Pooja says "I'm a lesbian."
Yash says "Your getting married tomorrow."
Suddenly Jenny was outside Yash's room listening to, their conversation and she goes to her room to tell Sonya.

Later that evening its Pooja's last night of freedom and she was in the lounge, with her mum and a few of her relatives have henna on their hands, she was sat on the sofa looking unhappy.
This occasion is when the bride's hands and feet are adorned with mehndi or henna. The girl's family and friends are also invited to have their hands adorned.
Sonya was standing there watching and Jenny stands next to her and she says "Are you ok."
Sonya walks off she is upset and Pooja looks at Jenny knowing why she was upset.
Sonya was upstairs and she was outside the terrace garden looking at the coloured lights hanging on the wall, it was making her mentally and physically ill, Pooja comes out and they both look at each other knowing that there love was coming to an end.
Sonya says to Pooja "My mum told me that you're going through with the wedding."
Pooja says to Sonya "I can't leave my family. Not now."

Lonely Love

Sonya looks angry and she says to Pooja "Keep your family."
Pooja says "My granddad found out about us. He told me to break up with you."
Sonya says "Then I should go."
Sonya looks away from Pooja and she goes inside, she walks to her room to get her suitcase.
Pooja was outside on the terrace and she stands there knowing, that she had no right to stop Sonya from going and she cries.
Sonya was in her room with her mum and they both had their suitcases ready to go.
Jenny says to Sonya "I don't understand why we are leaving?"
Sonya says "Pooja doesn't love me."
Sonya had tears in her eyes and Jenny couldn't bear seeing, her daughter suffering and she gives her a hug.
The next thing Sonya and Jenny were both downstairs with there, small suitcases ready to say goodbye to Asha and Dev.
Dev and Asha were both confused about Jenny and Sonya leaving all of a sudden.
Dev says to Jenny and Sonya "Why are you both going?"
Jenny says to Dev and Asha "I've had a call from my sister and she is ill."
Asha says "The wedding is tomorrow. Why doesn't Sonya stay."
Sonya says to Asha "My aunt needs me."
Dev says "Ok. Well if you both have time tomorrow do come."
Sonya didn't want to stay any longer and she says to Jenny "Mum we should go."
Sonya says to Dev and Asha "Bye uncle and auntie."
Dev and Asha say to Jenny and Sonya "Bye."

Lonely Love

Sonya and Jenny both walk off with their suitcases and they leave the house, as the front door was open for friends and relatives coming in and out of the house. Sonya was walking with her mum as they were both walking away from Pooja's house. Sonya's heart was beating and it was like Pooja, had cut it into small pieces and thrown it away, she could not help but to cry. They both stayed in a five star hotel, for the night and in the morning Jenny and Sonya catch a taxi to Delhi's main bus station.
Sonya and Jenny are both sat on the bench with their suitcases, as people were rushing in and out of the buses and waiting to go to their destination.
Jenny says to Sonya "Are you alright?"
Sonya says "I will never be alright."
Sonya takes a deep sigh and could feel, the pain and hurt that Pooja had caused her.
Suddenly Jenny sees Pooja walking with Dev, Asha and Yash and they were looking angry.
Jenny says to Sonya "Isn't that Pooja."
Sonya sees Pooja hoping to be with her, their plan might have not been a failure after all.
Sonya gets up from the bench and Dev, Asha, Yash and Pooja walk up to her.
Dev says to Sonya "How dare you."
Dev was so frustrated that he slaps Sonya on the face, Jenny jumps up from the bench, she pushes him away from her daughter.
Jenny says "How dare you slap my daughter."
Asha looks at Jenny says to her "Pooja told us this morning that she wants to be with Sonya. How can that be."
Jenny says to Asha and Dev "Let them be together."
Dev says "I won't let it happen. Pooja is getting

Lonely Love

married today. She is normal. I will make her normal."
Pooja gets upset Dev and Asha both walk off together with anger and disappointment.
Yash looks at Pooja and he says to her "Say goodbye to Sonya."
Yash turns around and he walks off towards the blue BMW car, where Dev and Asha were sat in the car waiting for Pooja.
Pooja goes closer to Sonya and they both look at each other, she folds her hands together at her.
Pooja says "I'm sorry Sonya. Please forgive me."
Sonya says "Go Pooja."
Sonya touches Pooja's face and she says "Take care."
Pooja puts her hands down and she turns around and she walks off, Sonya watches her walk out of her life forever.

Later in the day Pooja was at home and she was upstairs, in her room wearing her red glamorous bridle clothes she was sat on the bed, upset and she hated herself for being who she was, all she could think about was Sonya.

Asian gay females are treated appallingly due to their sexuality.
It depends on the country you live in; In India lesbians are treated very harshly.
If two lesbians are found flirty with each other they can be forced out of their accommodation.
Some girls find that due to their sexuality at school, they can face expulsion if they are found out.
Lesbians can suffer by being disowned by the family, outcast by the area they live in, beaten up and even killed.
This leads to such relationships being led underground

and out of sight or suspicion.
Rather than be open with the family, majority of such gay people will actually marry someone of the opposite sex, just to please the family and to ease the pressure off them.
In essence some marry to please the family but live another life, in private to fulfil their own satisfaction and needs.

Sonya and Jenny were both at Dehli airport waiting for the British airways flight, to arrive and to take both of them to New York.
While Sonya was standing next to her mother they were both looking hurt and upset, she couldn't stop thinking about Pooja's arranged marriage.

Is this the end for Sonya and Pooja's love for each other?

Will Pooja be brave enough to see Sonya again?

CHAPTER 7
THE WAY WE WERE

New York was missed by Sonya's love and happiness, but she had brought grief and sorrow back with her, she was at the embankment walking along the river she was feeling, disappointed and sad at how her life, had turned out she was all alone.
Later in the day Sonya was at her apartment in the lounge sat at the dinner table, trying to get over the pain that Pooja had caused her and she leans back in the chair, she takes a deep sigh she looked stressed as her heart was carrying a lot of sadness.

Will someone bring love and happiness for Sonya?

2 years had passed in New York City and Sonya was at the embankment and she was at her lunch break, she was working full time at a Bank in the city, it was paying her good money and she was happy there.
Suddenly Sonya hears Pooja's laugh and she looks to see where she is, right in front of her she sees a 29-year-old Asian man with black short hair and brown eyes slim build a handsome guy named Steve.
Pooja sees Sonya looking at her in shock and they were both staring at each other.
Steve says to Pooja "Who's that woman?"
Sonya turns around and she quickly walks off, trying to run away from her past but it kept haunting her.
Pooja looks at Steve and she says to him "That's Sonya."
The next thing Sonya was at her apartment and she shuts

Lonely Love

the front door looking distressed and upset, she was sobbing as she leans against the door Jenny comes out of her room, hearing her daughter crying and she goes up to her looking serious.
Jenny says to Sonya "What's happened?"
Sonya says "Its Pooja. She's here."
Jenny was shocked and she holds Sonya's hands and she says to her "Don't worry. Be strong I'm here for you."
The next thing Pooja was round Steve's two-bedroom house, which was near the city and they were both in the lounge sat on the sofa.
Steve says to Pooja "Are you going to see Sonya."
Pooja had to think about if it would be a good idea to see Sonya.
Steve says to Pooja "I think you should see Sonya."
Pooja says "She hates me."
Steve says "How do you know."
Pooja leans back on the sofa and she takes a deep sigh as she was confused about Sonya, Steve sits there trying to help her to go in the right direction.
Later that night Sonya was at her apartment and she was outside the terrace standing there, thinking of how and why Pooja had come to New York, it was causing her a lot of pain and emotional stress, she already felt lonely in her life.
The next morning it was about 11 o'clock Pooja arrives at Sonya's apartment, she knocks on the front door looking nervous.
Jenny opens the front door and she was surprised to see Pooja.
Jenny says "Pooja."
Pooja says "Hello auntie."
Jenny says "Come in."
Pooja walks in and she was scared of what Jenny might say

Lonely Love

to her.

Pooja says to Jenny "Is Sonya in?"
Jenny shuts the front door and she says to Pooja "No. Sonya is at work. But we can talk."
The next thing Jenny and Pooja were both in the lounge sat, at the dinner table drinking a glass of blackcurrant juice.
Jenny says to Pooja "Why have you come back?"
Pooja says "Because I still have feelings for Sonya."
Jenny says "So what happened when we left?"
Pooja says "I got married and then I told my husband the truth. He left me and I didn't go back to my parents."
Jenny was shocked and she felt sorry for Pooja and she wanted to help her.
Jenny says to Pooja "I don't know if Sonya wants you in her life. I don't even know if she still loves you."
Pooja understood that Sonya has moved on with her life.
Pooja says to Jenny "I should go."
Pooja gets up from the chair and she says to Jenny "Bye auntie."
Pooja leaves the lounge and she goes to open the front door and she leaves, Jenny is sat at her chair feeling stress and worried about the two of them.
The next thing Pooja is in the city and she is walking in the busy street, she felt angry and upset of what she had done but she wanted, to have a chance to talk to Sonya and to tell her that she still loved her.
Sonya was outside her workplace in the city and holding her black Gucci handbag in her hand, she was thinking about what to do with her, broken heart that Pooja caused 2 years ago.

Will Sonya visit Pooja?

Lonely Love

Later in the day Pooja was at her apartment in the lounge and she was sat on the sofa reading a fashion magazine, suddenly there's a knock on the door and she puts the magazine on the coffee table, she gets up from the sofa to answer the door and she knew it would be Steve.
Pooja opens the front door and she was shocked to see Sonya standing there.
Pooja says "Sonya."
Sonya says "Hi Pooja."
Pooja let's Sonya in and she shut the door and they both walk into the lounge, they were both looking nervous and afraid of what they might say to each other.
Sonya says to Pooja "How are you."
Pooja says "I'm fine. Did you miss me?"
Sonya doesn't look at Pooja's face and she says "I don't understand why I came here."
Pooja says "Because you still love me."
Sonya looks at Pooja and she says "I don't love you."
Sonya was hot tempered and she was ready to fight with Pooja, but the two stayed calm.

Will Sonya and Pooja both stay as friends?

CHAPTER 8
LOVE ME LOVE ME

It's the middle of summer and New York was trying to bring happiness to Sonya and Pooja, but they were both carrying hate and anger which was, not going away in there life.

Could there be love again?

It was a cold and windy Sunday afternoon Sonya and Jenny were both inside the coffee shop, sat at the table drinking a cup of hot coffee.
Jenny says to Sonya "I think you should give Pooja another chance."
Sonya says to Jenny "No way mum. I can't fall in love with Pooja again."
Jenny says "Why not?"
Sonya didn't want to get involved in Pooja's life again, she picks up her cup of coffee and takes a sip and Jenny looks at her daughter, knowing that she was being unreasonable.
Jenny says to Sonya "You can be her friend."
Sonya says "I suppose so."
Sonya looks at her cup of coffee and she puts it down on the table feeling miserable, she then thinks about her friendship with Pooja.

Two weeks later Sonya and Pooja were both walking in the park and they both seemed to be happy together.
Pooja says to Sonya "So we are friends."
Sonya says "Yes."

Pooja was happy and she smiles and she gives Sonya a quick hug.
Sonya was shocked the way Pooja behaved and she thought that she was being to friendly.
Pooja says to Sonya "I'm happy that you like me. Shall we go for lunch? Only if you want to."
Sonya says to Pooja "I would like that."
Sonya smiles at Pooja and they were both walking out of the park, they walk down the street to the bus stop where it takes them to the city.
Later that night Pooja was round Sonya's place and they were both in the lounge, sat on the sofa next to each other chatting, about their day out in the city.
Pooja still had feelings for Sonya and she couldn't help looking at her.
Pooja says to Sonya "I really like you."
Sonya looks away from Pooja and she realizes that their relationship wasn't going to work.
Sonya says to Pooja "You should go."
Pooja thought Sonya would have taken, her back and said to her that she wanted a relationship.
Pooja gets up from the sofa and she says to Sonya "Bye."
Pooja leaves the lounge looking gutted and she goes to the front door, feeling desperately disappointed and upset,
Sonya sits on the sofa waiting for her to leave. As soon as Pooja leaves, Sonya huffs and puffs and she had to get over her old love.
But Sonya couldn't understand why Pooja still wanted to be with her.
Pooja was outside Sonya's apartment and she walks in the street, having her arms crossed and she was feeling sad that Sonya was unhappy with her.
Sonya was at home and she was in her bedroom sat on the

Lonely Love

BED HOLDING A PILLOW CLOSE TO HER CHEST, SHE WAS UPSET WITH POOJA, SHE COULDN'T UNDERSTAND WHY SHE MET HER AND EVEN BEING HER FRIEND HAD MADE IT DIFFICULT FOR ONE ANOTHER.

THE NEXT DAY STEVE WAS AT HOME AND IT WAS HIS 30TH BIRTHDAY, THERE WERE A FEW MALE FRIENDS ROUND. POOJA WAS IN THE KITCHEN HOLDING HALF A GLASS OF WHITE WINE, STEVE WALKS IN AND HE SEES THAT SHE WAS LOOKING UNHAPPY.
STEVE SAYS TO POOJA "PARTYING ON YOUR OWN."
POOJA LOOKS AT STEVE AND HE SAYS "YOUR THINKING ABOUT SONYA."
POOJA SAYS "I THINK ABOUT HER DAY & NIGHT."
STEVE GOES TO THE FRIDGE AND OPENS THE DOOR TO GET A BOTTLE OF COLD COBRA BEER; POOJA SAYS TO HIM "DO YOU THINK I SHOULD CALL SONYA?"
STEVE SHUTS THE FRIDGE DOOR HOLDING THE COLD BEER IN HIS HAND AND HE PUTS IT ON THE TABLE, HE LOOKS AT POOJA AND HE SAYS TO HER "DON'T WAIT OR THINK ABOUT WHAT YOUR NEXT PLAN IS. JUST DO IT."
POOJA STANDS THERE LISTENING TO STEVE'S ADVICE HE WOULD ALWAYS, PUSH HER TO DO THE RIGHT THINGS IN HER LIFE AND SHE KNEW WHAT TO DO.
LATER THAT NIGHT SONYA WAS AT HOME AND SHE WAS WEARING HER WHITE SHORTS AND WHITE T-SHIRT, SHE WAS READY FOR BED WHEN THE DOOR BELL RINGS SHE THEN, GOES TO ANSWER THE DOOR AND IT WAS POOJA.
SONYA WAS SURPRISED TO SEE POOJA AT 11 O'CLOCK AT NIGHT AND THEN SHE THOUGHT THAT SHE MIGHT HAVE BEEN IN TROUBLE.
SONYA SAYS "HI POOJA."
POOJA SMILES AT SONYA AND SHE SAYS TO HER "HEY BABY. CAN I COME IN."
SONYA LET'S POOJA IN AND SHE SHUTS THE DOOR, IT WAS CAUSING HER STRESS SEEING HER.

Lonely Love

Sonya turns around to look at Pooja.
Pooja says to Sonya "I want to tell you something."
Sonya was looking at Pooja and she wanted her to leave because whenever she saw her, it reminded her of the pain and hurt she caused her in the past.
Pooja says to Sonya "I love you."
Sonya was horrified and she stands still, she gets angry with Pooja and she says to her "What's your game!"
Pooja says "There's no game Sonya. I really like you."
Sonya looked furious and she says to Pooja "You should go."
Pooja says "I'm not going. I'm staying here for the night."
Pooja smiles at Sonya and she goes into her room hoping that she would follow.
Sonya was tired of Pooja's affection for her and she walks into the lounge and she sits on the sofa, she turns to look at the window watching the night sky, it was like she knew that someone was trying to make her fall in love with Pooja again.
But Sonya was not having it, so she lies on the sofa telling Pooja that she wasn't interested.

The next morning Pooja was in Sonya's room lying on the bed asleep, suddenly the sound of her mobile ringing next to her wakes her up, picks it up to answer the call and it was, Steve and she suddenly she falls off the bed.
Sonya was in the kitchen waiting for the kettle to boil so she, can make a cup of tea and Jenny walks in and she says "I've just heard a noise in your room."
Sonya says "Its Pooja."
Jenny looks at Sonya and she was excited that they were back together.
Sonya says to Jenny "Pooja came round last night."

Lonely Love

Jenny says "So your both."
Sonya looks at her mum and she didn't look happy with Pooja being there.
Sonya says to Jenny "No we are not seeing each other. I slept on the sofa."
Suddenly Pooja walks out of the bedroom and she quickly goes to the kitchen, where she sees Sonya and Jenny standing there.
Pooja says to Jenny "Hi auntie."
Sonya opens the top cupboard to get a cup and she looks at Pooja.
Sonya says to Pooja "Do you want a cup of tea?"
Pooja says to Sonya "No thanks. I have to go."
Pooja goes up to Sonya and she gives her a kiss on the cheek and she leaves the kitchen.
Pooja says "Bye auntie."
Sonya stands in the kitchen holding the empty cup in shock and Jenny giggles at her, they both hear the front door shut.
Jenny says to Sonya "I see Pooja was being extra nice to you."
Sonya ignores her mother and she puts the empty cup on the table and she leaves the kitchen, she then walks into the lounge and she goes outside, the terrace to see Pooja walking in the street.

Has Sonya finally got feelings for Pooja?

Will Pooja win Sonya's heart?

CHAPTER 9
LOVE IS IMPOSSIBLE

As the days go by in the month of September, summer was coming to an end in New York City.

Is there a chance for Sonya and Pooja being together?

Steve and Pooja were both in the city; they were walking in the street.
Pooja says to Steve "What was it that you've been trying to tell me."
Steve was looking happy and excited about something and he says to Pooja "I'm getting married."
Pooja looks at Steve and she was happy for him and she holds him, as they were both walking in the street she says to him "Congratulations."
Steve says to Pooja "Her name is Neha. She's wonderful. So tell me about you."
Pooja says "I don't want to get married. I'm a lesbian. I was married and that failed."
Steve says "No silly not marriage. You and Sonya."
Pooja says "I really like Sonya. I love her. And I've told her but."
Steve looks at Pooja and he was trying to give her hope and support and he says to her "You will be with Sonya. She's just scared of telling you how she really feels about you. She doesn't want to lose you again."
Pooja was listening to Steve; she knew that he was right about how Sonya felt towards her.

As Pooja and Steve both walk down the street it soon

Lonely Love

Became evening.
Steve was at home and he was having a party with a few of his male and female friends, Pooja was outside the back garden, she was trying to call Sonya but there was no answer.
Sonya was at her apartment and she was in the lounge her mum, Ravi and Rani they were sat at the dinner table.
Rani says to Jenny and Sonya "Its my daughter's best friends wedding next week. And you two are invited."
Jenny looks at Sonya and they were both not up to going to a wedding.
Jenny says to Sonya "Shall we go?"
Sonya says "Yeah why not."
Ravi was pleased that Jenny and Sonya were going and she says "Great."
Rani looks at Sonya and she was afraid of saying something to her, as it still freaked her out about homosexuality.
Rani says to Sonya "So do you have a girlfriend?"
Sonya looks at Rani and she thinks, she was making fun out of her and she takes it serious.
Sonya says to Rani "No. Why do you have a girl for me?"
Ravi and Jenny both look serious and they keep quite.
The next thing Sonya was outside the terrace garden and she was sat on the bench, she takes a deep sigh of sadness she feels lonely, she wanted to be loved by a woman but it wasn't going to be Pooja.

A week later it was Steve and Neha's wedding and it was held in a small hall in Manhattan.
The wedding reception party is virtually the first public appearance of the couple together.
Pooja sees Sonya standing with her mum, Ravi and Rani and she goes to them.

Pooja says "Hi auntie and Sonya."
Pooja looks thrilled to see Sonya and she couldn't wait to talk to her.
Sonya says "Hi Pooja."
Rani looks at Ravi and Jenny and she says quietly to them "That must be Sonya's girlfriend."
Sonya looks at Rani, Jenny and Ravi and she gets annoyed with them, whispering behind her back and Pooja looks at them and she says "I'll see you all later."
Pooja walks off and Jenny gets annoyed with Sonya's attitude and she says to her "You could have been nice to her."
Jenny pinches Sonya's arm and they both look at each other.
Sonya says to Jenny "Mum."

Later in the day after the wedding ceremony Steve and Neha, both received the blessing and gifts from friends and relatives, in the hall where the stage is set at the wedding reception area, is adored with exquisite and magnificent decorations, as for Sonya she wasn't really happy being there, seeing Pooja had made her feel down and stressed.
Sonya sees Pooja's happiness for her dear friend Steve and walks off in a huff leaving Jenny, Ravi and Rani going to congratulate the newly weds.
Jenny looks to see where Sonya was going and she says "Now where is that girl going."
Rani and Ravi both look at Jenny's distressing face knowing where Sonya has gone.
Rani says to Jenny "Sonya has probably gone weak seeing her girlfriend."
Jenny gets annoyed with Rani's silly comments about Sonya, she ignores it and gives her the cold shoulder.

Lonely Love

Sonya was outside the hall and she stands there taking some fresh air, she was thinking about her friendship with Pooja weather to take it any further or not, even though she still had feelings for her.

Later that night Pooja was at her apartment and she was in her bedroom, taking off her gold bangles of her right hand, she puts them in the draw when the door bell rings she thought it was odd for someone knocking, on the door at 11.30 at night and she leaves the bedroom, she goes to open the door she is shocked to see Sonya standing there.
Sonya says to Pooja "Hi. Can I come in?"
Pooja says to Sonya "Yeah sure come in."
Sonya walks in and Pooja shuts the door and she turns to look at her.
Pooja says to Sonya "So how come you're here?"
Sonya says "I wanted to talk to you."
Pooja says "Firstly would you like tea or coffee?"
Sonya says "Coffee please."
Pooja walks in to the kitchen and Sonya follows her.
Pooja says to Sonya "I didn't see you in the evening."
Pooja goes to the top cupboard to get an empty cup, Sonya looks at her and her heart was beating for something she wants.
Sonya says to Pooja "I really like you."
Pooja is shocked and surprised to hear Sonya had feelings for her; she had been waiting for this moment to happen.
Pooja looks at Sonya and she says to her "You do have feelings for me."
Sonya goes closer to Pooja and she touches her hair and they both gaze into each other's eyes, they both could feel that there was an attraction and desire, for one another and they have a passionate kiss.

Lonely Love

The next thing Sonya and Pooja were both in the room in the bed cuddled up to each other asleep.

The next morning Sonya was in the bedroom and she was wearing her red sari, from last night and she was sat on the bed putting on her gold sandals on, she then gets up from the bed and she leaves the room.

Sonya quietly walks to the front door not making any sound, Pooja was standing in the lounge and she sees her and she goes up to her.

Pooja says to Sonya "Where are you going?"

Sonya looks at Pooja and she says "I'm going home. My mum's waiting for me."

Pooja smiles and she gives Sonya a kiss on the cheek and she looks at her and she says "I'll see you later."

Sonya says "Ok."

Sonya opens the front door and she walks out and Pooja shuts the door, feeling happy and in love that she was back with her.

The next thing Sonya was in the city walking in the street, it was a windy cold day she sees a church in a another street, she quickly crosses the road as there was no cars coming and she walks to the church and she goes inside, there she sees an old man with white short hair and hazel eyes and wearing, a brown jumper and black trousers and black shoes and he was sat there saying his prayers.

Sonya walks to the front and she goes to light a candle and she folds her hands, she shuts her eyes praying to get an answer from God with her life.

Sonya then opens her eyes and she puts her hands down and she turns around, she leaves the church as she steps out it was raining and she walks outside, she looks up at the cloudy sky and she could feel, the rain fall on her face

Lonely Love

It was like god wanted her to decide for herself.
Pooja was at her apartment and she was outside the terrace garden feeling happy and excited, she was dancing in the rain, it was like her love had finally come back to her, this time it was going to last forever.
The next thing Sonya was at her apartment and she was wearing her jeans and a white v-neck jumper, she was in the lounge sat on the floor near the fireplace and she was feeling cold, as her hair was wet from the rain.
Sonya was sat on the floor thinking about Pooja and how, happy she was and she takes a deep sigh.
Pooja was at her apartment and she was in the lounge wearing jeans and a red v-neck jumper, she was sat on the floor near the fireplace, she was drying her hair with a small white towel.

Will Sonya & Pooja be together forever?

Or has Sonya got other plans in her mind?

LONELY LOVE

CHAPTER 10
YOU AND ME

It's near the end of Pooja and Sonya's story is there a happy ending for the two of them?

Has New York filled the colours of love and happiness for Sonya and Pooja's life?

It was a Friday afternoon and Sonya had a day off from work, she was round Pooja's place and they were both standing near each other in the lounge.
Sonya looks tense and she had something to say to Pooja, but she didn't want to hurt or upset her.
Pooja could see Sonya's face that she looked anxious and worried about something.
Pooja says to Sonya "Are you alright? Why are you sad?"
Sonya looks at Pooja trying keep cool and calm and she says "I'm not sad."
Pooja goes up to Sonya and she holds her hand for support, she could see that she was not happy.
Pooja says to Sonya "Talk to me."
Sonya had enough of Pooja being caring and loving towards her, she then gets agitated by her.
Sonya says to Pooja "Ok fine. I don't love you. I did love you once but that was in the past."
Pooja was shocked and horrified and she lets go off, Sonya's hand it was like her heart had been ripped apart.
Pooja thought Sonya wanted to spend the rest of her life with her.
Pooja says to Sonya "I thought you still loved me."
Sonya says "I'm sorry."

Lonely Love

And they both hear the rain from outside the terrace garden.
Sonya turns around and she leaves the lounge and she goes to the front door, Pooja stands still not knowing what to do or say she had never been so upset.

As soon as Sonya left the apartment Pooja cries and she turns around and walks outside, the terrace garden where it was raining she stands there, she covers her hand over her mouth so no one could hear, her cry not even the heavens could help her broken relationship.
Sonya was walking in the street with her arms crossed feeling the rain, falling on her she was wet and cold while walking alone, in the street after hurting Pooja. Later that night it was still raining in New York City it
was like, the heavens were crying with Sonya and Pooja.
Sonya was at home and she was in the lounge and she was standing in front of the window watching the rain, she was feeling low and depressed she thinks about her next, move in her life she knew that there was, no trust in love and friendship with Pooja.

The next morning the rain had stop and it was a cloudy and windy day in the city, Sonya was at home and she was sat at the dinner table, wondering what to do and if it would be a good idea to see Pooja again.
Jenny walks in the lounge, she sees her daughter looking unhappy and she goes up to her.
Jenny says to Sonya "Have you upset Pooja?"
Sonya looks at her mum and she couldn't believe that she knew her problems.
Jenny says to Sonya "Why did you do that? I thought you wanted to be with her."

Sonya says "I did but Pooja wanted to get married and be with her family."
Jenny says "You can still be with her."
Sonya says "I want to move away."
Jenny was shocked that her daughter was running away from her past and she tries to help and support her.
Sonya says to Jenny "You can stay with your brother."
Jenny was heart broken that Sonya was leaving without her.
Jenny says "Will I see you again?"
Sonya holds her mother's hand and she says to her "Of course you will. I will come and see you every month."
Jenny says "Your running away from Pooja. But how long are you going to run for?"
Sonya lets go off her mum's hand, she gets up from the chair and they both look at each other.
Sonya says to Jenny "All you need to know is that I love you mum."
Sonya holds Jenny tight in her arms to ease the pain she feels in her troubled and confused life.

Later that evening Pooja was at her apartment feeling depressed, she was in the lounge lying on the sofa thinking about what Sonya had said to her, it made her feel mentally and physically ill, there's a knock on the front door and she sits up from the sofa and she gets up and leaves the lounge, to answer the door and it was Jenny looking sad and stressed out from Sonya problems.
Jenny says "Hello Pooja."
Pooja says to Jenny "Hello auntie come in."
Jenny walks in and Pooja shuts the door knowing it was about Sonya and they both look at each other.
Pooja says to Jenny "Shall we go to the lounge."
Jenny walks into the lounge and she goes to sit on the sofa and Pooja stands near the fireplace.

Lonely Love

Jenny says to Pooja "I'm sorry that Sonya broke your heart."
Pooja keeps her emotions away from Jenny and she was strong about what Sonya said to her.
Pooja says to Jenny "I thought Sonya wanted to be with me."
Jenny says "I should tell you this. Sonya is leaving New York."
Pooja was shocked and she couldn't understand why Sonya was leaving.
Pooja says to Jenny "Are you happy that your daughter is leaving you."
Jenny says "No. But I know why Sonya is running away because she loves you."
Jenny knew that her daughter was making a wrong mistake in her life.
Pooja says to Jenny "She doesn't love me."
Pooja had tears in her eyes and Jenny could see how upset she was, she gets up from the sofa to give her a hug.
Sonya was at her apartment sat at the dinner table with the Sony, laptop booking a one-way flight ticket to Australia on the net. She leans back in her chair and she takes a deep sigh of sorrow.
Jenny was at the embankment walking on the bridge and she looks at the river flowing forwards and backwards, she couldn't keep up with Sonya's problems and it was, causing her deep emotional stress and she has tears in her eyes.

As the sun was going down in New York City it soon became dark and dull.
Sonya was at home with her mum and they were, in the lounge both sat on the sofa, next to each other holding hands, this was there last moment of living together as

Lonely Love

Mother and daughter.
Jenny couldn't help but to cry for her daughter's grief but, there relationship was never going to end even though they would be far away from each other.

As the sun rises for the last time for Sonya in, New York she was going to be missed by the heart-warming, city leaving her all alone in a different location.

Will Pooja stop Sonya from going?

Sonya was at home in her room packing her clothes and underwear into a large dark purple suitcase that was, on the bed she was feeling sad that she was, leaving her mother's warmth and love and she had tears in her eyes. The next thing Sonya walks out of her bedroom with her suitcase, in one hand taking it to the front door and Jenny walks, out of the kitchen looking upset and she goes up to her.
Jenny says to Sonya "Have you got everything."
Sonya says "Yes mum."
Sonya and Jenny both go up to each other, they both hold each other as they were deeply going to miss each other.
Sonya and Jenny both look at each other.
Sonya says to Jenny "I'll phone you everyday."
Jenny says "You will come back and see me."
Sonya takes her mother's hand close to her face and she says "I promise that I will come see you."
Sonya and Jenny both give each other a hug and they cry for one another.
Pooja was at the embankment walking alone and she was thinking, weather to see Sonya and if there was a chance for the two to be together.

Lonely Love

Will Pooja have enough time to save her broken love?

Later that day Sonya is at the airport and she has her brown handbag, on her shoulder and she was holding her flight ticket and passport in one hand.
Suddenly Pooja quickly walks inside the airport and her heart was racing, for her lost love and she tries to see where Sonya is.
Sonya turns around she sees Pooja looking for her and she goes up to her.
Sonya says "Pooja. What are you doing here?"
Pooja looks at Sonya and she says to her "You're making a
big mistake."
Sonya gets angry and annoyed with Pooja being there to get her, thinking that she will fall in love with her again.
Sonya says to Pooja "I made a mistake meeting you. I told you not to get married."
Pooja says "But I left my husband and family because I knew I wanted to be with you. Please give me another chance."
Sonya says "No chance. Goodbye Pooja."
Sonya turns around and she walks to the departure area and Pooja is stood, there knowing that she had moved on with her life.
Sonya had every right to leave because Pooja had hurt and caused her pain in her life.
Sonya had no room to have Pooja back in her life not now not ever.

The next thing as Sonya's plane leaves grieving New York City.
Pooja is walking in the street and it was a cloudy cold day as she is walking in the street, she was looking sad

Lonely Love

And miserable she had her head held down, it suddenly starts to rain it was like New York, could feel the pain she was going through and she couldn't help, but to cry and it starts to rain even more with her, as she was crying for grief and regret in her life.

Jenny was at home and she was in the lounge sat on the sofa looking at a photo of Sonya, she was already missing her daughter and she gets upset, as she touches the photo with great sadness.

Later that night Pooja was at her apartment in the lounge, she is sat near the fireplace holding a photo of Sonya and she rips it up, with anger and she takes a mournful cry of sorrow.

There love came to an end and they both went there separate ways. But it didn't mean that they both didn't fall in love again.

They thought that there love would last a lifetime but it didn't. They tried so much to hold on to their relationship, hoping that they would be together but Pooja and Sonya were both left with lonely hearts.

And as for Jenny she was living alone in New York, crying and yearning for her daughter to come back home.

LONELY LOVE

www.ingramcontent.com/pod-product-compliance
Lightning Source LLC
Chambersburg PA
CBHW071414040426
42444CB00009B/2237